FARTING BETTER

When your ass is used to farting, you can't keep it quiet! The best guide on how to fart perfectly. Farting like no one's ever done before..

From an Incredible Effort of the Grandmaster

MAO TZE TZE

Table of contents

INTRODUCTION

Have you ever been in a situation where farting would be extremely embarrassing, and you have had to hold back a fart? Admit it, we've all done it.

Trying to hold back farts leads to a build-up of pressure and severe discomfort. A build-up of intestinal gas can trigger abdominal distension with some gas being reabsorbed into the circulation system and exhaled. Holding farts for too long means that the accumulation of intestinal gas will eventually be released through an uncontrollable fart.

It is not clear whether increased pressure in the rectum increases the chances of developing a condition called diverticulitis, in which small sacs develop in the intestinal lining and become inflamed or whether it does not matter at all.

So what is flatus?

Flatulence, farts and farting refer to intestinal gas that enters the rectum due to the body's normal gastrointestinal processes of digestion and metabolism and then exits through the anus.

As your body digests food in the small intestine, components that cannot be broken down move further along the gastrointestinal pathway and finally into the large intestine called the colon.

Intestinal bacteria break down some of the contents by fermentation. This process produces gases and products called fatty acids that are reabsorbed and used in metabolic pathways related to immunity and prevention of disease development.

The gases can be reabsorbed through the intestinal wall into the circulation system and finally exhaled through the lungs or excreted through the rectum, like a fart.

How many farts are normal?

It can be difficult for researchers to convince people to sign up for experiments that measures farting. But luckily, ten healthy adults volunteered to quantify the amount of gas they release in a day.

Over a 24-hour period, all the farts they released were collected via a rectal catheter (ouch!). During the experiment, participants ate normally, but to ensure a boost in gas production they were also asked to eat 200 grams of baked beans.

Participants produced an average total volume of 705 ml of gas in 24 hours, ranging from 476 ml to 1,490 ml per person. The largest volume produced was hydrogen (361 ml in 24 hours), followed by carbon dioxide (68 ml/24 hours). Only three adults produced methane, which ranged from 3 ml to 120 ml/24 hours. The remaining gases, thought to be mainly nitrogen, contributed about 213 ml/24 hours.

Men and women produced about the same amount of gas and had an average of eight episodes of flatulence (individual or a series of farts) over 24 hours. The volume varied between 33 and 125 ml per fart, with greater amounts of intestinal gas released during the hours after meals.

The gas was also released while they slept, but at half the rate during the day (average of 16 ml/hour compared to 34 ml/hour).

Fibre and flatulence

In a study on dietary fibre and flatulence, researchers investigated what happens to intestinal gas production when people a eat a diet rich in fibre.

The researchers invited ten healthy adult volunteers to follow their usual diet for seven days, consuming 30 grams of soluble fibre per day. They were asked to add 10 grams - about a tablespoonful - to each meal over the course of a week.

At the end of each week, the participants were taken to the laboratory and, in a carefully controlled experiment, an intra-rectal catheter was inserted to quantify how much gas (in terms of volume, pressure and number) moved through the intestines over a couple of hours.

It was discovered that the high-fibre diet led to a longer initial retention of gas, but the volume remained the same which meant fewer but longer farts.

Where do farts come from?

The gas in the intestines comes from several sources. It may be due to the ingestion of air. Or from carbon dioxide produced when stomach acid mixes with bicarbonate in the small intestine. Or the gases may be produced by bacteria found in the large intestine.

While these gases are believed to perform specific tasks that have an impact on our health, the production of excessive intestinal gas can cause bloating, pain, borborygmus (meaning noises in the intestines) and several farts.

The smelliest farts are due to sulphur-containing gases. This was confirmed in a study involving 16 healthy adults who were fed borlotti beans and lactulose, a non-absorbable carbohydrate that gets fermented in the colon. The odour intensity of the flatulence samples was assessed by two judges (unfortunate for them).

Le Petomane:
The world's most
famous fartist

Before we continue our scientific discussion of the mystery that is farting, we would like to introduce a unique talent, a model, an inspiration to you: Le Petomane.

Of all the stars on the stage in the cultural Mecca of late 19th century Paris, the biggest attraction at the Moulin Rouge was a man who was farting.

The farting man, Joseph Pujol was called Le Petomane, meaning 'The Fartist', and proved to be the epitome of the artistic fart. Pujol's unique ability to control his farts offered a style of comedy that transcended age, ethnicity, gender and time.

In 1892, Pujol appeared before an audience at the famous Moulin Rouge, impeccably dressed in a red coat, black satin trousers and white gloves, and announced: 'Ladies and gentlemen, I have the honour to present a session of Petomanie. The word Petomanie means someone who can fart at will, but don't worry about your nose. My parents wrecked themselves smelling my rectum. "

Le Petomanie began by targeting young boys, imitating a bride on her wedding night (with a very small fart). A long ten-second fart replicated the sound of a seamstress ripping two metres of fabric. Then, with all his might, he would explode one in the form of a cannon shot.

"People were literally writhing," one journalist wrote, *"Women, stuffed into their corsets were taken away by nurses the shrewd manager was stationed in the lobby."* Fortunately, the smell was not a concern for the nurses. Le Petomane kept his farts completely odourless by undergoing an enema before each performance.

Biographers Jean Nohain and F. Caradec recount the story of Le Petomane's life in their 1967 book, Le Petomane in 1857-1945. As the book reveals, Pujol discovered his unusual talent as a child during an annual family outing to the beach. While playing underwater and holding his breath, the boy suddenly felt a cold sensation in his stomach. Alarmed by this strange sensation, he ran off to a private place to investigate. Almost two litres of water began to pour out of his backside. After this gastrointestinal geyser, he visited a doctor, who merely laughed and advised him to stay away from the sea. Pujol did not think about the event again, at least not for a while.

Years later and while recounting the incident to his friends on the beach, Pujol was urged to see if he could still create similar water magic with his bottom. And he could. Thrilled by his friends' reaction, Pujol began to develop his talent by practicing with air instead of water. Before long he could suck in air and blow it at will in the form of a nice, clean fart. In a biography reproduced in the book Le Petomane, his son described the process as a 'real fart fantasy'.

Pujol adopted the name Le Petomane and shared his gift with the public by renting a stage in his hometown of Marseille. He quickly became a local sensation. Word of mouth was more than enough in his ascent to fame and he needed no publicity. Before long he was performing in other provincial towns and achieving similar success. Le Petomane was ready for the big time, so he filled up his tank and headed for Paris.

In the early 1890s, the Moulin Rouge became famous thanks to its lively cabaret, fast-paced Cancan shows and famous actors such as Sarah Bernhardt. But when Le Petomane arrived at the theatre and met director Charles Zidler, he presented himself as the latest 'phenomenon' of Paris. He would become famous, he reassured Zidler, throughout the city. Zidler's curiosity was aroused. *"What exactly is your expertise?"* He asked. According to an article in the Moulin Rouge archives, the conversation went as follows:

Le Petomane: *Well, you see monsieur, I have an anus that works like a suction device. In other words, my anus is so elastic that I can open and close it at will.*

Zidler: *So?*

Le Petomane: *So, monsieur, through this fortunate opening, I can suck out any amount of liquid that is given to me.*

So Zidler offered a large tub of water to Le Petomane. Pujol came prepared with a hole in his underwear and quickly sucked the water out of the tub and let it flow back in.

Then Le Petomane continued his demonstration:

Le Petomane: *That's not all! After this kind of enema, I can continuously expel odourless gas. The secret of my performance lies in the different qualities of sound I can produce.*

Zidler: *So, you sing from behind!*

Le Petomane: *Yes, monsieur, tenor, one! Baritone, two! Bass, three! Alto, four! Soprano, five! Now, a singer, that's it!*

Zidler: *And my mother-in-law, can you imitate her too?*

Le Petomane: *That's it!*

(There was a deafening noise.)

Zidler: (laughing to the point of tears) *You're hired. You are starting tonight.*

Zidler did not realise that Le Petomane would become the most profitable act at the Moulin Rouge. His performances brought in 20,000 francs per show, more than twice as much as Bernhardt's.

Apart from his impersonations, Le Petomane also performed other acrobatics on stage. The innovative Pujol inserted a rubber tube into his backside and a cigarette at the other end, which he smoked by contracting his anal muscles to draw the smoke in and out. After extinguishing the cigarette, the master would transform himself into a flatulence flautist. By connecting the instrument to the pipe he was capable of playing pieces such as 'Le Roid Dagobett' and 'La Marseillaise'. To complete his rectal repertoire and to end his show in dramatic fashion, Pujol would demonstrate his true lung power by blowing out a candle from a metre away, then extinguishing the gas lights on stage one by one.

Once again, just like in Marseille, Pujol had become so popular that it was time to find a new audience to appreciate his virtuosity. Le Petomane then took a leave of absence from the Moulin Rouge and travelled through Europe and North Africa. When Pujol returned, he had grown accustomed to his independence and chose to open his own variety theatre. The Moulin Rouge was angry at his sudden departure and staged a competitive act: La Femme Petomane named Mademoiselle Thiebeau. The idea that another fartist could replace Pujol was absurd, and she was quickly exposed as a fraud.

In 1914, when the First World War began, Le Petomane retired from the theatre and instead ran a bakery in Marseilles, then a biscuit factory in Toulon. He died in 1945 at the ripe old age of 88. But even in his later years he continued to practice his anal hygiene. "'Every morning after going to the toilet he gave himself an enema using about two litres of hot water'," his son wrote, "and was therefore always thoroughly clean".

Unlike other farts, which exist only for a brief stinky period before fading into nothingness, Pujol's farts have become immortal. In addition to the book Nohain and Caradec, Le Petomane is also the focus of several films: a 1979 biographical film called Le Petomane, starring Leonard Rossiter; a 1983 Italian film called Il Petomane; and the 1998 documentary, Le Petomane: Fin de Siècle Fartiste.

Le Petomane did not want to be misrepresented, so there are only a few seconds of film depicting his act. Unfortunately, they are all soundless.

Now that you know, your farts could always be a plan B as far as your career is concerned, you might be even more fascinated. Therefore, after entertaining you for a while, let's now get back to us. What should you know about farting?

Everything you need to know about farts

"Ouch, my ass is burning like fire! What does that even mean? Maybe it's the poo that wants to come out? Yeah, yeah, shit I know it, I can see you, I can hear you...And... E... What's that? Is that possible? Oh gods! My ear, you don't deceive me? Nay indeed, it is so. What a very long and sad sound!"

Wolfgang Amadeus Mozart

What does flatulence mean? Where does it come from? The word 'flatulence' is derived from flato, from the Latin word flatus which means 'breath', a word with an Indo-European root that indicates a swelling or filling. This term is not usually used in the spoken language and instead popular, dialectal or vulgar terms are used. It should not be confused with meteorism, which is a meic condition in which gases are not passed out and thus back up into the gastro-intestinal tract, causing various problems, including bloating in the abdomen.

The most common term - fart and its regional variants, come from the colloquial expression of the act of 'farting'. This term originates in turn from the act of " loosening" the correggia, which in Latin expresses the term corium = leather, an ancient term for the belt of trousers, thus signifying the release of gas; there is also a second hypothesis, according to which the term is derived from the Greek word, kor-kor-y-ghe, an ancient onomatopoeia, indicating the bubbling, or even the sound of intestinal gas.

The word 'peto', and the variants 'petto', and 'petta', are apparently derived from the Latin word peditum, from the verb pedo, in turn from the Proto-Italic *pezdō ('petare'), from the common Proto-Indo-European root *pesd-, which appears to be onomatopoeic.

2.1 Why do we fart?

"Let's not forget that even Romeo and Juliet occasionally farted and scratched their asses."

Carles Simic

Flatulence, also known as farting, is a phenomenon that everyone experiences. In fact, everyone releases gas formed by digesting the food they eat. This gas inhabits the entire digestive tract, including the stomach, small intestine, colon and rectum.

So, we fart because of the accumulation of gas in our bodies which is usually due to:

- Ingested air: we ingest air during the day, including complex drinks or intake of air while chewing.

- Bacteria in the small intestine: there are a number of reasons why bacterial overgrowth may occur, including type 2 diabetes, coeliac disease, liver disease and inflammatory bowel disease.

- Carbohydrates ingested are not digested properly: it happens that food is not digested by the enzymes in the small intestine properly. When this happens, the carbohydrates get into our colon, and are converted by bacteria into hydrogen and carbon dioxide gas.

Where does this extra gas then go? Some of it is absorbed by the body, but if this gas becomes too much, it can cause severe pain in the stomach and chest. So, the gas is released through our back door, we no longer feel pain, and the pain will be felt by others in our presence when we fart!

2.2 Why do some people fart so much?

"Most people like to read their own writing and smell the stench of their own farts."

W. H. Auden

Sometimes you may notice that you fart more than usual. The increase in farts produced may be a natural response by the body, although sometimes there may be a medical reason. Factors that can influence the amount of farting include:

- The time of day

Ingesting a lot of gas-producing foods during the day may cause an increase in flatulence in the evening. In addition, you will fart more when the muscles in your intestines are stimulated, such as when you are about to go to the toilet. Exercising a lot or coughing a lot can also cause increased flatulence.

- The food you eat

Some foods are known to make you go to the toilet more frequently, others make you fart a lot, while others cause constipation. Traditionally, foods such as beans, broccoli or roughage will cause increased flatulence, but not all of these foods will have the same effect on different people. Therefore, our advice is to learn about your body so that you know which foods to avoid in order to reduce your flatulence.

- Pregnancy

Pregnancy is a wonderful time in a woman's life, yet she also has to put up with some not-so-pleasant changes, such as an increase in flatulence. This is due to hormonal changes in the woman's body, which cause a slowdown in digestion and therefore an accumulation of gas in the intestines.

- Menstruation

Hormonal changes that occur during a woman's cycle can also cause changes in the bacteria in the digestive tract, and consequently, increased flatulence.

- Health conditions

Diseases in your digestive system can cause you to produce more gas. Even surgical operations on the intestines may cause bacterial overgrowth and the subsequent production of more intestinal gas.

2.3 Why are some farts silent and others noisy?

"Women and farts slip out even if you don't want them to."

Stefano Benini

Everyone farts. In fact, a person farts an average of about 14 times a day with an average volume of half a litre of gas per day, says Michael Rice, M.D., a gastroenterologist at the University of Michigan Medicine Gastroenterology Clinic.

That's a lot of air. But every fart you release isn't exactly the same. In fact, some are quite easy to hide, while others, let's say you can hear them from the next room.

So why do your farts make different noises? And is there anything you can do to turn a loud fart into a silent fart?

First of all, farts depend on many variables, including what you eat, drink and the movements of your body as the gas is released.

"As food is digested, gases including carbon dioxide, methane and hydrogen build up in the intestines and look for their way out," says Dr Rice.

The intestines contract and move their contents, including gas, through peristalsis, or rather, contractions that move waste through the digestive tract, towards the anus. Small gas molecules join into larger gas molecules on the way out and when your body releases those gases, they result in a fart.

The sounds of your farts depend on the vibrations produced when the gas exits your anal canal, says Dr

Rice. Despite popular belief, fart noises have nothing to do with the flapping of your buttocks.

"The sounds of farts are very much shaped by the speed at which they are expelled, as well as the shape and size of the anal sphincter that opens as they pass through," says Dr Rice.

He likens it to a musical instrument: the smaller the size of the exit point, the higher the pitch and perhaps the more squeaky it will be. The larger the opening at the moment, the smaller the sound.

"There are probably many factors that determine the overall anus size at the time a fart comes out, including the overall resting pitch of the anus and other behavioural factors," Dr Rice states. "You can manipulate the fart sound by relaxing and tightening the external anal sphincter and diaphragm to change the tone, volume and length of the sounds."

The anal sphincter tightens in a similar way as you would if you were trying to hold in poo, and because the opening would be narrower, this could lead to a squeakier, shorter fart (which is why you like the smell of your own farts).

And the rate of expulsion, or the speed at which the air leaves the body, also plays a role. If the air comes out faster, your fart is more likely to be louder.

Also, if the ingested air triggers your farting as is the case with most farts, they tend to be noisier (but less smelly), Dr Rice says. If your fart is mainly driven by digestion and bacterial fermentation, it will tend to be smaller in volume and sound, but smellier.

In most cases, whether your fart is loud, quiet or smelly, there is really nothing to worry about. But there are some times when your farts may signal a medical problem.

"Consider seeing a doctor if your farts are symptoms associated with fecal incontinence, frequent involuntary passage of gas, persistent abdominal discomfort, abdominal distension, or blood loss," Dr. Rice says.

Your doctor may ask you about your diet, bowel movements, family history or other medical conditions and examine you to determine if you may have a medical condition that requires further evaluation or treatment, such as irritable bowel syndrome (IBS), ulcerative colitis, colon cancer or other gastrointestinal conditions.

2.4 Why do some farts feel warm?

"Just as there is no salad without vinegar, there is no urine without farting."

On average, each of us farts 14 to 23 times a day. Most of the time, this happens while you're sleeping, so you don't notice it. However, other times it happens during the day, and these farts come in different types: silent, smelly, loud or even painful.

You may even feel that your farts are warm or that there is a feeling of warmth in your backside as they are expelled. In reality, the temperature of farts never changes, but there are other factors that cause this sensation.

What causes the sensation of warm farts?

On average, the temperature of farts is always the same. The feeling that your farts are hotter than normal can happen for several reasons:

- The scarcity of farts

No one will ever complain about not farting enough. Yet, when you fart very little, the few gas emissions that are made can feel hotter than normal. As we have already seen, the amount and type of farting we experience depends largely on our lifestyle.

However, farting less can cause the familiar sensation of warmth. This is due to the fact that when farting, we expend more effort. In doing so, our anus is strained more and therefore causes this unnatural warm sensation.

Otherwise, if we fart more, we may not notice this warm sensation: the gas will be released with less effort and therefore will not cause any exertion.

- Dysentery

If you are suffering from diarrhoea, or are going to the toilet very often, you may experience a sore anus or the skin around it may become slightly sensitive. In this case, you will feel a sensation of heat, due to the state of the skin and the anus.

- Spicy food

When you eat spicy food, your farts may feel a little warmer than normal. There is nothing strange about this, as spicy foods contain substances that can cause this slightly uncomfortable sensation. For example, capsaicin, which makes food so spicy, could be the cause of your warm farts.

In reality, the farts will no longer be warm, but again the anus will be irritated by these spicy substances contained in the food you have ingested - and then expelled as gas - and thus cause the warm sensation.

- Tight trousers

Wearing tight-fitting trousers can mean that the farts will stay closer to your backside for longer and therefore you may experience that warm feeling.

- Constipation

Constipation is another one of those factors that can cause the feeling of warmer-than-normal farts. This is for the same reason as explained above, i.e. the effort you put into releasing the extra air will cause the much-discussed warm feeling.

If you are trying to get rid of constipation, you will need to make some lifestyle changes. For example, you will need to eat more fibre, drink more water, or exercise more.

These are the main reasons why you may feel that your farts are warmer than normal. But what can you do if this feeling is bothering you and you want to get rid of these farts?

How to get rid of the warm fart feeling

As we said, farts are not " warmer " than others, at least not usually, but because of a number of reasons related to your lifestyle and what happens inside your body when you get rid of excess gas. So let's look at what we can do to avoid this unpleasant feeling and to help you with any stomach pains.

- Fibre, fibre, fibre!

Fibre is the go-to for anyone looking to improve the functioning of their gastrointestinal system. In fact, fibre intake reduces the likelihood of constipation and helps regulate bowel movements.

So, we could say that fibre is responsible for everything that comes out - in solid and gaseous form!

However, keep in mind that some foods rich in fibre will have the opposite result: they will cause an increase in farts. However, the farts won't feel warm, so if you're willing to put up with a little extra gas, you'll get rid of the unpleasant feeling of warmth.

- Long live Probiotics

Probiotics contain bacteria that will utilize nutrients within the stomach and intestines, such as fibre, and then release small particles of hydrogen.

However, other probiotics do exactly the opposite, i.e. they can reduce the amount of gas inside your body, and therefore the amount of gas that will come out of your backside. Foods that can help with this are yoghurt, pickles and kombucha.

- Use more spices

Spices can be your allies in this regard, as they contain natural enzymes and chemicals that can help your gastrointestinal system. For example, ginger, mint and cinnamon can calm your intestines, and reduce problems such as diarrhea or skin irritation.

- Fewer carbohydrates

Your stomach can't process all the food you ingest. For example, foods containing insoluble fibres are too complex for our stomachs to break down. Despite this, the stomach always tries and in doing so, creates gas that accumulates in the gastrointestinal tract. This then results in a greater quantity of fart products.

This does not mean that you should stop eating all types of carbohydrates - quite the opposite! Many foods that are good for your health contain quite a few carbohydrates. Think of fruits and vegetables such as apples, beans, cabbage and onions. So instead of eliminating all sources of carbohydrates, instead try to choose the best types of carbohydrates and limit your consumption of 'bad' carbohydrates.

The chemistry of farts

"Those who judge based on their stomachs confuse meteorism with the voice of instinct."

Sosio Giordano

Farts are often considered to be funny or embarrassing, and they certainly are, but they are also vital to our health.

The unpleasant smells of farts are a minor inconvenience when you consider the risk of explosion that a build-up of unreleased gas could cause. Complex carbohydrates such as fibre from our food that pass undigested through our small intestines could be converted into over 13 litres of highly flammable hydrogen per day.

It is astonishing that this potential danger is not publicised more widely and perhaps even more astonishing that doctors and scientists try to use it to diagnose diseases.

Surely we can't produce that much hydrogen or we'd all get blown away! So what happens? Intestinal bacteria come to our rescue!

Intestinal bacteria swallow hydrogen, fortunately for all of us. Up to two kilograms of microorganisms inhabit our colon, fermenting the approximately 40 g of complex carbohydrates each day. Bacteria in the colon can produce about a 1/3 litre of hydrogen per gram of carbohydrate, which equates to over 13 litres per day. But the microbial mass is effectively a refinery that converts partially digested food into substances that often affect our health, in which the hydrogen produced by Firmicutes bacteria is also a raw material.

For example, some bacteria react the hydrogen with sulphate ions and produce hydrogen sulphide gas, which not only smells rather disgusting, but is itself flammable. Archaea microbes can also lower the flammability level by reacting between four hydrogen molecules and one carbon dioxide molecule to form one methane and two water molecules.

So, after all this chemistry, what gases are in our farts and in what quantities?

Most of the gases we release from our bowels are odourless, up to a quarter are simply oxygen and nitrogen from ingested air. Although - as you may have heard - farts differ greatly from person to person, about three-quarters are carbon dioxide, hydrogen and methane that are produced by our intestinal flora. According to gastroenterologist Michael Levitt of the Minneapolis Veterans' Affairs Medical Center in the

US, only a third of us have a flora that generates methane. Since the 1970s, Levitt has led the way in determining the composition of intestinal gas, sometimes inserting tubes into patients' rectums to collect their farts.

In 1998, Levitt's team used rectal tubes for a detailed study of the composition of farts in six healthy women and 10 healthy men for four hours. The total gas released by the individuals ranged from 106 ml to 1657 ml, but only four released methane, and the largest fart produced over half a litre of hydrogen. And Levitt's team's measurements suggested that even the smelly components did not use much hydrogen. Collectively, hydrogen sulphide, methanol, which smells like rotten cabbage and dimethyl sulphide, similar to garlic, averaged only 50 ppm of each fart.

So how many farts is that?

"I'm a professional, I'm never late... and I try to keep the flatulence under control."

Donald Surtherland

In four hours, the 16 individuals farted between three to nine times, with an average volume of 100 ml per fart. That frequency is well within the range that

Rosemary Stanton and Terry Bolin of the University of New South Wales in Australia also observed in healthy people in 1998.

Stanton explains that they studied farts because "they found that people avoided many foods containing fibre because they believed flatulence was a sign of poor digestion". They asked 60 men and 60 women to count their farts and monitor their food intake. The men farted between 2 to 53 times a day, with an average of 12.7, while the women farted between 1 to 32 times a day, with an average of 7.1. The number of farts was higher when people ate more fibre. The study shows that farting is normal, Stanton says. "I hope this has resulted in people being ready to eat more foods rich in dietary fibre."

How can the gases produced in our intestines reveal anything about our health?

"During an interview I was asked what my worst defect is and I answered 'flatulence'. That's why I have my own office."

Dan Thompson

There is evidence that imbalances in intestinal microbes linked to irritable bowel syndrome (IBS) and other diseases cause changes in hydrogen and methane levels, says Ben de Lacy Costello of the University of the West of England in the UK. It is possible that methane may contribute to constipation, as it appears to inhibit intestinal muscle contractions known as peristalsis.

Similarly, hydrogen sulphide may stifle muscle contraction and is linked to intestinal wall damage and possibly even inflammatory bowel disease and colon cancer. However, there are questions about the usefulness of the test because many people produce a lot of hydrogen and methane for a variety of reasons that are difficult to identify. And Levitt says he doesn't believe methane production has anything to do with an irritable bowel.

Consequently, De Lacy Costello and his colleagues went beyond the most common gases to study volatile compounds released from faeces in very low concentrations. Initially, they simulated conditions in the large intestine by mixing faeces and nutritional medium in a container. They absorbed volatile chemicals onto plastic fibres above the mixture, to be analysed by gas chromatography coupled with mass spectrometry. The team found 297 compounds, including volatile sulphur compounds and molecules such as indole and skatole, which are often linked to faecal odour. They also found other compounds with a more pleasant odour, including alpha- and beta-pinene and limonene. The patterns of these compounds differed between healthy people and those with ulcerative colitis or infections that cause diarrhoea.

Pinene and limonene??! Then why don't your farts smell like pine and lemon?

Even at very low concentrations compounds such as indole, skatole and sulphur compounds dominate the odour of other compounds.

What is the best way to control farts?

"We are here on earth to walk around farting. Don't let anyone tell you otherwise."

Kurt Vonnegut Jr.

"Don't hold them for too long - it produces distress in susceptible people," Stanton says. "Avoiding fibre may reduce gas production, but fibre is important for many reasons: it reduces the risk of colorectal cancer, haemorrhoids and diverticula. Soluble fibre in oats and many fruits and vegetables promotes the growth of 'good' bacteria in the colon. The bacteria then produce short-chain fatty acids that are absorbed by the colon and help reduce serum cholesterol and blood glucose levels. "

So as long as the farts aren't causing you physical pain, you then those around you might have to learn how to turn the other cheek.

How can I stop farting so much?

"There's more talent in the smallest of my farts than there is in your whole body.

[Speaking to Barbra Streisand]."

Walter Matthau

Farting might be a source of embarrassment to some, but it's a normal consequence of digestion. No matter what anyone says, everyone does it, and it's a sign that the digestive system is working properly.

It is normal for excess gas to be released, and if it wasn't, it would cause serious health problems and unbearable pain.

As mentioned above, we all fart between 5 to 15 times a day. Does that sound like a lot? It isn't! Most of the time it happens at night, and many other times the farts are silent, so we don't even notice them.

You should know that if you feel like you are farting all the time, it is probably because you are aware of your farts, unlike most people. It is normal to eliminate 0.5 to 1.5 litres of gas per day.

Farting a lot should not be something to worry about. It is true that some people do it more than others, but this does not mean much about the person's level of health.

However, if a person feels that their farts are becoming uncontrollable and therefore feels particularly embarrassed and uncomfortable, there are a few things they can do to try and reduce the amount of unwanted air from their backside. Let's look at which ones.

- Drink water

You get the idea. The simple act of drinking water helps a lot with bowel functioning, and consequently helps against excessive gas, as being constipated can cause more farts. As for the amount of water to drink, this varies from person to person, because someone who does sport, for example, will need to drink more water. The ideal amount to drink is 30 to 40 ml per kilo, i.e. if you weigh 50 kg, for example, you should drink between 1.5 and 2 litres per day.

- Eat slowly and without talking

Do you like to eat while watching TV or sliding your fingers across the phone screen? Do you like to chat with friends while chewing? Know that this interferes with your digestion. When you eat very quickly, due to stress or anxiety for example, too much air can enter your body, which causes gas to form. In addition, ingesting air during meals leaves you with a bloated belly and encourages increased burping.

- Eat foods that are easy to digest

Some foods, mainly carbohydrates, proteins and fats are slightly slower to digest and increase fermentation in the intestines, leading to gas formation. The main foods responsible for excess intestinal gas are:

- Cabbage, broccoli, cauliflower, corn, milk;

- Chickpeas, peas, lentils, potatoes;

- Beans, sweet potatoes, yoghurt, eggs, wheat bran;

- Carbonated drinks, beer, onions, asparagus.

Combining high-fibre foods with foods containing a lot of fat also promotes gas formation, so you should avoid eating whole-meal bread with cheddar cheese, for example.

However, a food that may cause gas in one person may not cause it in another, so if you notice gas forming, try to remember what the food was that caused it and avoid it.

- Do not take antacids or antibiotics

The use of antacids and antibiotics can alter the intestinal flora and, therefore, the process of fermentation of micro-organisms. Thus, there is an increased production of intestinal gas.

- Physical activity

Lack of physical activity slows down the digestion process, increasing the fermentation of food. In addition, sedentary people tend to suffer from constipation, which also encourages the formation of intestinal gas due to stools remaining in the intestine longer.

- Avoid drinking fizzy drinks

Carbonated drinks make it easier to swallow more air, so eliminating carbonated drinks can greatly improve the need to eliminate excess gas.

- Try to go to the toilet often

If stools remain in the intestines for longer, they increase fermentation and make it difficult for gas to be released, so it is advisable to stop constipation by making changes to your diet.

- Massage your tummy

You know when a child has colic or gas and the parents massage their tummy? Well, abdominal massage can help a lot to eliminate gas, even for adults. Just follow the gas path through the large intestine, making clockwise movements. It helps in the elimination of gas and in fighting constipation.

- Chewing gum

As mentioned earlier, talking and 'swallowing' increases gas production. So when you chew gum, you are ingesting air all the time. It is also bad for your stomach because the organ understands that there is food coming in, even though it is not actually there. For this reason, it produces more gastric juice, which can harm those who have problems such as gastritis.

- Ginger consumption

In addition to having anti-inflammatory and antioxidant properties, ginger also stimulates gastric emptying, which aids digestion and the swelling of the upper digestive tract. They use it a lot with people who suffer from dyspepsia (chronic indigestion), which causes discomfort in the upper stomach. It also prevents faeces from remaining in the intestines. How to consume ginger? Taking it in capsules may be a good idea for better absorption, but grating it and putting it in a salad and/or making a tea are also good options. Remember that anything in excess can be bad.

- Taking probiotics

Probiotics are bacteria that aim to rebalance the intestinal flora, ensuring that it functions properly. Probiotics can be found in milk-derived and fermented foods, such as yoghurt. They can also be taken as supplements, but always under medical advice.

- Eat less legumes

Beans, chickpeas, soya, lentils: legumes are known to cause flatulence. Since they are healthy foods, it is best to keep them in your diet, but always leave them to soak in water for about 12 hours. This eliminates the phytates, an enzyme inhibitor that hinders the digestive process.

4.1 Solving your constipation problems

You may suffer from constipation due to excess gas in the intestines. In fact, when stools remain in the colon for too long, they continue to ferment in the body and thus produce gas that will have to be released somewhere and will smell very bad.

As for treatment, there are several treatments. Start by drinking lots of water and eating fibre - these are two of the things that work best in these cases.

You can also try using medications and emollients, which you can find in pharmacies or online.

Here are a few suggestions that may help

- Eat small and frequent meals

- Chew slowly and for a long time

- Exercise regularly

- Make sure your diet is regular and healthy

- Try drinking mint tea, which can help digest and soothe your tummy

- No smoking of cigarettes or sweets

- Do not wear tight-fitting clothes

- Avoid foods that are difficult to digest

If a person is having difficulty because their farts are too many (or too smelly) they can - and probably should - contact a pharmacist or doctor. They may recommend different solutions: for example, did you know that there are special underwear and tampons that absorb odours?

Preventing gas build-up may simply be a matter of diet. For example, if you think you are intolerant to dairy products, you will clearly want to avoid foods that contain this substance.

As we've already mentioned, avoid fizzy drinks, carbohydrates, eat small portions and replace hard-to-digest fibre-rich foods with highly digestible, light foods.

When do you have to worry about your farts?

"Trump of the ass, sanity of the body."

If you fart more than the average - which as we said is 15 farts a day - then you may be farting excessively. If this is the case, you should visit your doctor, and investigate whether you are suffering from gastrointestinal problems.

This is especially important if you suffer from pain caused by cramping, bloating, or similar symptoms.

Consider that conditions such as irritable bowel syndrome, Crohn's disease, celiac disease, lactose intolerance and peptic ulcers are all associated with excessive flatulence.

The best way to fart

"We are here on earth to walk around farting. Don't let anyone tell you otherwise".

Kurt Vonnegut Jr.

Why would anyone want to fart more, you might ask? It' s very simple! Because farts are fun, they can be a unique way to win an argument or an effective way to make someone who's bothering you leave. Or maybe you want to perform a little show for your friends, or you're thinking of pursuing a career like Le Petomane. Whatever the reason may be, farting more and doing it differently is certainly possible.

Clearly, the fastest and most effective way to fart in style is through your diet. In general, beans, fibre-rich grains, fruits and most vegetables (especially cauliflower and broccoli) work for most people. The most impressive results are often achieved in the first week of switching to a vegetarian diet from a meat-based diet.

After that, the results will diminish as your body gets used to the new diet. But during that first week, you can expect to produce copious amounts of gas, resulting in an impressive 100+ farts per day.

There are two types of foods to consider when it comes to farting successfully: those that will help you with volume and those that will help you with the smell.

The former will help you increase the amount of gas produced. So much that you'll get a bellyache. But not nearly enough and you won't be able to hold the pressure needed for a good long fart. And what about the auditory gratification and satisfaction of your audience?

In turn, the more pungent the smell, the more likely it is that those around you will suffer from the smell of the fart. This is what will give you olfactory gratification and nasal satisfaction.

Consider that due to individual differences in body chemistry (digestive enzymes, bacteria, etc.), these food products may not work the same for everyone. Experiment to fine-tune what works best for your physiology.

Here is a list of the best foods to fuel your farts:

- ω   Apples
- ω   Apricots
- ω   Beans
- ω   Bran
- ω   Broccoli
- ω   Brussels sprouts

ω   Farting Better   Mao Tze Tze

ω   Cabbage
ω   Carrot
ω   Cauliflower
ω   Dairy products
ω   Aubergines
ω   Peanuts
ω   Onions
ω   Peaches
ω   Pears
ω   Popcorn
ω   Plums
ω   Sultanas
ω   Soya beans
ω   Tuna fish

Sulphur is the secret sauce!

"I knew how to appreciate a good fart, whether it was mine or someone else's."

Bill Bryson

A little chemistry lesson. The gas that really makes farts unpleasant is hydrogen sulphide (H_2S). Hydrogen sulphide is known as the rotten egg gas. Our bodies will create more of this gas when we mix foods high in sulphur with foods high in hydrogen because these foods provide the raw ingredient to form H2S.

Since high-sulphur foods are what provide the key ingredient, it is worth knowing what they are.

- Meat is one of the best sources of sulphur because one of the key ingredients found in amino acids within meat is sulphur. Chicken, turkey, beef, pork, rabbit, most fish and goat are all very rich sources of sulphur in meat.

- Eggs are an excellent source of sulphur. Hen eggs, especially the yolks are rich in sulphur.

- The Allium food group includes spices such as chives, onions, garlic, leeks and shallots. These foods contain compounds such as allyl sulphides and sulphoxides, making them one of the best sources of sulphur!

- Vegetables contain glucosinolates which are sulphur-rich nutrients. Edamame beans are the richest in sulphur. Vegetables high in sulphur are other beans, peas, sweet corn, spinach, broccoli, cauliflower, cabbage, bamboo shoots, asparagus, turnips, aubergines and lettuce.

- Avocado is a fruit (yes, it's a fruit, not a vegetable!) with the highest sulphur content, followed by kiwi, bananas, pineapple and strawberries. Grapefruit, melons, grapes, peaches and oranges are also high in sulphur.

- Other foods high in sulphur include chocolate, milk, dairy products, tea, coffee, cereals, cashews, sesame seeds, pistachios, peanuts and other nuts.

Now, if you don't want to radically change your eating habits, here are some recipes that will help you make the ideal fart.

Recipe n.1

Ingredients:

- ω   Whole eggs (ideal in terms of volume are the whites, but if you want to get a really disgusting smell, choose whole eggs. The sulphur in the yolks will make all the difference).

- ω   Borlotti beans

- ω   Rice

- ω   Whole wheat tortilla

- ω   Soy milk

Directions:

Fry the contents of at least three eggs, mix with a can of borlotti beans and some rice, roll in a whole wheat tortilla and down it all with a large glass of soy milk.

Wait for a couple of hours and you'll be amazed at the show!

Recipe n. 2

Ingredients:

- ω   Vanilla protein powder mixed with warm milk.

- ω   4-6 slices of wholemeal bread

Directions:

This recipe is really simple and quick to make. Don't let its elegant simplicity deceive you, for some people it could be the beginning of the end.

Recipe n. 3

Ingredients:

- Protein shake (any flavour, mixed with milk)

- Baked beans, steamed cabbage, broccoli and Brussels sprouts.

Although quick to prepare, don't underestimate the rampage this little beauty can unleash in your bowels.

ω   Farting Better   Mao Tze Tze

Recipe n. 4

Ingredients:

- ω   Baked beans

- ω   Broccoli

- ω   garlic

- ω   Eggs

- ω   Protein bar (the sugar alcohols inside will provide that extra edge) or protein shake with milk.

Directions:

This is a wolf in sheep's clothing. It doesn't appear to be a lot, but there is a real beast lurking beneath the surface, just waiting for you to release its stench with your digestive juices.

Recipe n. 5

Ingredients:

- ω   Brussels sprouts

- ω   Cabbage

- ω   Beef with mushrooms

ω   Farting Better   Mao Tze Tze

ω   3 grams of sulphur powder or tablets

Directions:

Once again, don't let simplicity be mistaken for ineffectiveness.

<u>Recipe n. 6</u>

Ingredients:

ω   Glucose

ω   Liquorice powder

ω   Whey powder

ω   3 grams of sulphur powder

ω   A glass of warm milk

Directions:

Proceed with caution. Just do a small test meal before attempting a big blast. Don't say I didn't warn you! If all goes well the first time, to add to the adventure and excitement, next time you could increase the quantity to two portions (two glasses).

Some useful tips

-   Chewing gum is a great way to improve your farting skills because it stimulates your digestive system and makes you swallow more air than usual.

-   Of the three main nutrients (protein, carbohydrates, fat), carbohydrates produce most of the gas because starch and sugar ferment easily. About 50% of the world's population have bacteria that specifically prefer to munch on unprocessed carbohydrates. As you may already know, beans contain more indigestible carbohydrates than most foods.

-   Many everyday foods are considered 'indigestible' - milk being one of them for people who are lactose intolerant. Lactose intolerance means that the body is unable to digest the milk sugar, so it sets it aside as waste. If you are lactose intolerant and have a lot of 'gaseous enzymes' in your digestive system, milk will be a fantastic fart refuel for you.

-   Because of differences in the composition of each person's intestinal fauna; people do not necessarily react in a similar way to the same foods. For example, 2 people may eat a meal rich in indigestible carbohydrates and one of them may generate gas. This is because their intestinal tract contains more enzymes. This explains why one person may claim that apples or onions make them fart, while others may claim not to be affected. It depends on the type and amount of bacteria in the large intestine.

5.1 Tactical positions for farting

"You can't fart without changing the balance of the universe."

Philip K. Dick

Now, we will be learning something else, which can be combined with the teachings of the previous chapter. These positions are borrowed from yoga, but in our case, they will be useful for getting rid of irritating air, or for creating the primordial fart: the fart of destiny, if you prefer that.

No one will be able to get close to you... they will only be able to stay away from you!

Through this technique, you will be able to fart at will. And for the best results, prepare one of the recipes mentioned in the previous chapter.

Although the first part of the book is much simpler than what you are about to learn, these techniques will help you release farts worthy of a fart master, a gas king, a prophet of the air. Your farts will be loud, long, and above all, forthcoming without too much effort.

You will never be bored again! You might feel embarrassed, but not bored. Plus, you'll have something unique to entertain your friends with.

So let's look at how to learn these simple techniques. In the practice of yoga, positions or postures are known as Asanas.

While you are in one of these positions, try to relax the muscles around your abdomen and buttocks. When you do this correctly, you will feel a small, steady stream of air enter your lower back. Holding your nose and breath at the same time will let the air in faster. Using your free hand to separate one of your butt cheeks will also help a lot.

After a few seconds of "breathing in" like this, your body will have the urge to expel the air, and you will fart.

Don't be discouraged, because this technique requires a lot of practice. Most people do not succeed at first. But don't give up! People who master this technique can let out the most outrageously long and loudest farts you've ever heard! I'm talking 30 to 90 seconds and more.

As you develop your skills and understand how to perform the technique, you will no longer need to engage in the showy positions you are about to learn. You will enter 'invisible' mode and be able to fart on command while sitting or standing, and will therefore be able to surprise people anywhere and at any time!

And at this stage you can take your skills to the next level by combining the foods you learned in the first part with the physical technique you will learn in this chapter.

What are the best positions?

"Urinating without farting is like playing the violin without the bow."

Yoga is not a mystical, spiritual or paranormal activity that releases blocked energies, it is simply a series of exercises with an emphasis on stretching. Yoga is actually also an activity that can strengthen important muscles involved in digestion and can help relieve flatulence-related bloating and reduce farts or, at least, help you fart in a more controlled way. In fact, it works so well that many people are afraid to fart during yoga classes.

You may find it helpful to do some of the yoga exercises below to reduce gas and enable you to fart in private instead of in group sessions, or to practice in private so that you can release them in public. Check it out!

- Pavanmuktasana means release from the air and, as the name suggests, can be helpful with stomach gas problems.

Lie on your back and raise your right knee to your chest. Interlace the fingers of both hands on the top of the knee to keep it on your chest. Now raise your head and try to touch your knee with your nose. Hold your breath and stay in this position for 10-20 seconds, then relax and stretch your leg.

Repeat the above with your left knee, then with both knees held to your chest and try to place your nose between your knees.

Repeat all the above steps three or four times. Did you feel the flatulence fluttering out?

- Halasana helps to make the spine more flexible. Halasana also improves the strength of the muscles and nerves in the spine, and is an effective exercise for the waist and massages the digestive system to alleviate flatulence problems.

Lie on your back with your legs and feet together and your arms along your sides, with your hands by your thighs. Keep your legs straight, inhale slowly and lift your legs to 30 degrees, 60 degrees and 90 degrees with a pause at each stage. As you exhale, push your legs higher, above your head and then continue until they reach the floor without bending your knees.

Extend your legs as much as possible so that your chin rests firmly against your chest. Then raise your hands and try to hold your toes and maintain that position for a few seconds to three minutes, depending on your ability and comfort level, while breathing normally. Finish by slowly performing the previous steps in the reverse order.

- Dhanurasana is a yoga pose that strengthens the abdominal organs and provides relief for constipation and excessive flatulence.

Lie face down with your arms stretched across your body and legs straight. Bend your legs at knee level, bringing them forward so that you can firmly grasp your ankles with your hands. As you inhale, extend your legs backwards and lift your thighs, chest and head off the floor at the same time. Your arms should be straight and the weight of your body should be on your navel.

Your knees should be kept close together and the position should be maintained for a few seconds while holding your breath. Release the breath and the queuing farts will be released instantly.

- The happy child yoga pose is great for relieving gas

Lie on your back and as you exhale, bend your knees into your stomach. As you inhale, grasp the outside of your feet with your hands. If you have difficulty reaching your feet with your hands, a loop belt over each foot may be helpful. Spread your knees a little wider than your torso and move them towards your armpits.

Place each ankle directly over the respective knee so that the shins are perpendicular to the floor. Gently push your feet into your hands or the loop belts as you lower your hands to create resistance. Move your thighs towards your body and the floor as you stretch your spine. Maintain this position for half a minute to a minute, then place your feet back on the floor as you exhale.

Now that you know which positions will help you fart freely, and which will help you become a fart master, practice them until you take control of your backside. Your power will be infinite!

5.2 Final advice

"Dreams and farts remain in bed."

For those who want to take this skill to the next level and start entering and winning fart contests, here are some tips.

Allow them to ferment. Don't let them out as soon as you feel them coming. Many people fall into this trap. They simply let their farts seep slowly whenever they feel them coming. You have to give them time to ferment, to build up the pressure.

The fermentation process will achieve highly desirable results:

1) The fart will be much smellier. Just like a good wine needs time to age, you need to ferment your farts. They need to be cultivated, coaxed and nurtured. Give them the time and attention they deserve at this delicate stage. Help them to develop their full potential.

2) It will increase the pressure. This will allow you to do much more damage. It will greatly increase your versatility. For example, you will be able to release much longer farts.

3) It will allow you to be much louder and have more control over your tone and volume. What's the point

of farting if no one can hear you? Some compositions will be amplified thanks to a microphone, but I would recommend practicing without one.

The higher the tone, the better. This will travel much further and can be heard above most noises, even in a crowded noisy environment, such as a classroom. Low tones are good if you want to make a minor statement, but for important announcements, the higher the better. To get the highest tone, you'll need to practice on how to keep your anus closed as tightly as possible, while at the same time forcing gas through it. If done correctly, it will chirp like a bird. With practice, you will be able to play a tune. Start with something as easy as Fra Martino Campanaro, before moving on to challenging classics like the 1812 Overture.

The art of hiding farts from your partner

If you can fart in front of your better half, the romantics often remark, it's a sign that you've found your soul mate.

That doesn't mean it's true. Farting is disgusting and no one, not even the love of your life would want to be within 15 metres of you when you let one slip. Maybe this entire line of thinking is just something guys made up so they could feel justified in farting around their girlfriends?

All of this is a rather long-winded way of saying that if you fart a lot, dating your partner for long periods of time can be difficult. Can it happen that you sneak off for a fast blast when she or he isn't looking? Then you will know that there are cases when this is not possible. Over time, you'll be able to perfect some pretty foolproof techniques that men and women can use to secretly - and safely - fart around their partners. Or in fact, anyone else you'd prefer not to notice your farts.

- Farting on the pavement

The pavement fart is particularly useful for silent but deadly farts. Depending on the level of ambient noise

- traffic, noisy subways and so on - you can probably try a moderate volume fart. This technique works best when the wind is blowing against you: even the most powerful farts will quickly leave your vicinity when the gas is released, exonerating you immediately.

If the wind is not in your favour, blame it on the smell rising in the air. But don't be the first person to point this out: you know the old children's rhyme, right? Before you commit the act, take a quick look behind you to make sure no one is walking in your wake. This is a courtesy and a way to avoid embarrassment. You don't want to be seen as a fartist, even by a stranger.

- The cough fart

A risky proposition for those unfamiliar with the intricacies of their gastrointestinal tract, the cough fartis not for everyone. You need to have a feeling for the power of the fart before you release it. If you're going to squeak one and cover it with a cough, it better not smell like the inside of a boar's digestive tract. But if you know, depending on what you've eaten and how your stomach feels, that the fart will be relatively low on the stink scale, then the cough fart is there for you.

Be careful, though. The fart should never be louder than the cough! This is extremely difficult to control ... as the cough causes the fart to leave your anus with more force than you would expect. So it's helpful, but it involves a greater degree of difficulty.

- Farting under the covers

If you experiment with this technique for a while, you will find that even the most pungent flatulence goes unnoticed if you do it right. (Warning: use a duvet, a thick barrier between your fart and your nose. If you sleep only with a sheet over you, we cannot guarantee the reliability of this method). Make sure that your partner does not lift the blankets for about five minutes after you release one.

The gas stays there longer than you would imagine, as anyone who has farted under the sheets and then gone under it for a quick whiff knows. Farting under the covers is best for quiet farts, which, in my experience, often come in the morning when you don't want to disturb yourself by getting up and going to the toilet.

- Farting in the bathroom

Farting in the bathroom works magnificently if you don't overuse it. Your better half will be suspicious if you sneak away to the toilet every 10 minutes to have a fart. She'll probably start to think you have more stomach problems than some gas floating around in there. Anyway, it helps if you have to pee, in which case you can flush the toilet just as you're carrying out the act.

Bathrooms don't hide as much noise as we think, so if you can also turn on the fan and maybe the sink, then all the better. Throw in a cough too, just to be on the safe side. Make sure your partner doesn't come in right after you and try to leave the door slightly ajar so the room can gradually air out.

- The fragmentary fart

If done well, this is one of the most efficient techniques. You need to know that you are capable of releasing the fart in fragments until it is completely out of your system. It can't be so big that it comes out completely when you start squeezing. (Those are best for the bathroom.) If you let it go a little here, a little there, over the course of five or 10 minutes, no one will notice.

This method is most practical when you're having dinner, preferably out at a restaurant, so your better half can't notice what's going on under the table as you carefully flex your sphincter to let go of the gas. Remember that your facial expressions can give you away. Take a sip of your drink when you're about to release one so that your face is partially hidden.

- Farting in the kitchen

Fish, bacon or anything else with onions will help mask any scent. If you're inviting your partner over for dinner, choose one of these foods or something else with an aroma that permeates your home for a while. It will confuse the scents and no one will know if that smell is gas or food - or both. Not to mention that your better half will be so enthralled that you made dinner that they won't even notice that the pungent smell might be from a fart.

- The trapped fart

The trapped fart is the riskiest technique of all and should be used sparingly. It is useful for car journeys when you have no other choice (and rolling down the window would be suspicious), or for when you are cuddling on the sofa and prefer not to kill the vibe. (However, keep in mind that farting will kill the vibe way more than getting up to go to the bathroom).

I would recommend practicing this a couple of times before trying it in front of your partner. It doesn't always work, especially since it requires some dexterity with your buttocks to seal the fart underneath you. To do this, sit up straight, press your butt, hard, into the seat and join your legs together. You will want to direct the fart slightly to the front of you so that it does not escape from the butt.

Then, let it out slowly and quietly and wait for the verdict.

Interesting facts
about farting

"When the ass is used to farting, you can't keep it quiet."

1. The average human being farts about 14 times a day.

How many times they do it in front of others will determine exactly how "human" - actually, "inhuman" - they are.

2. You fart enough every day to fill a balloon.

The average human being produces about 700 ml of flatulence a day, enough to blow up a birthday balloon!

3. What exactly is a fart?

Flatulence occurs in almost all living organisms and is a mixture of hydrogen, nitrogen, oxygen, carbon dioxide, sulphur dioxide and, in some cases, methane. These gases are produced as a by-product of the trillions of bacteria that break down food during the digestive process.

4. Can farts be measured?

Yes, indeed, it is possible: using a 'rectal catheter', researchers have been able to push a tube into a patient's anus to determine the volume of gas produced during the sacred act of farting.

5. The speed of farts.

Farts leave the anus and enter the world at a rate of 3 farts per second, or just under 12 kilometres per hour.

6. What the hell is that smell?

Actually, only 1% or less of the gas in your ordinary, everyday fart stinks. The main culprit is hydrogen sulphide, which generates those rancid "rotten egg" scents that make farts the bane of the world's nostrils.

7. Women's farts smell worse than men's farts.

Sure, there are a number of people who think it's funny to fart in front of others, and to be honest, women don't tend to be among those people. But before challenging a woman, men should realise that women's farts have a higher concentration of hydrogen sulphide than men's and therefore, fart for fart, they are smellier than men's farts.

8. *A fart with any other name would have the same smelly smell.*

The word 'fart' is considered a foul word and, just like the fart itself, is not recommended for its use in polite company. The polite name is 'flatus', although most people hardly use it. The word 'fart' is said to have been coined in 1632 and defined as 'letting the wind out of the anus'. I don't know where "wind" comes from because it's not very often that the smell of wind makes you want to vomit.

9. *Farting in ancient times.*

The Roman emperor Claudius declared that "all Roman citizens should be allowed to fart whenever necessary", which is an ancient variant of the modern maxim, "Wherever you are, let the fart come freely". The ancient Japanese were said to have held 'farting contests' to see who could do it loudest and longest. The Greek physician Hippocrates decreed that "Farting is necessary for well-being".

10. The oldest joke in recorded history is a fart joke.

Professor Paul McDonald of the University of Wolverhampton describes a Sumerian joke from 1900 BC as the oldest recorded joke in the world.

11. Farts are scattered throughout literary history.

Despite our modern revulsion at human flatulence - it is such an unspeakable subject, it may qualify as a form of pornography - the literary masters of antiquity did not suffer from such blockages. Literary luminaries who mentioned farting include William Shakespeare (flatulence is mentioned five times in his plays), Jonathan Swift (who wrote a 1722 essay titled 'The Benefit of Farting Explained'), Geoffrey Chaucer (whose Canterbury Tales include a line about a man who "made a fart as loud as thunder"), Dante Alighieri (whose Inferno mentions a demon who used "his anus as a trumpet"), and founding father Ben Franklin, who wrote an entire essay entitled "Fart Proudly".

12. Hitler farted a lot

Not only was the infamous Nazi dictator a maniac, but he also suffered from hepatitis and gastrointestinal cramps, which led to a condition of chronic flatulence for which he took 28 different medications. It is almost certain that no one complained to Hitler about the smell.

13. *Would you like a low-flatulence 'legume snack'?*

A food engineer named Massoud Kazemzadeh obtained a patent in 2001 for "low-flatulence legume snacks" that supposedly contained the nutrients of a bean without any unpleasant bloating.

14. *OK, so how about some anti-flatulence underwear?*

A manufacturer known as Shreddies makes underwear with "charcoal-lined pads" designed to reduce the offensiveness of your flatulence,

15. *There are pills that can make your farts smell like chocolate or roses: take your pick.*

A Frenchman named Christian Poincheval was disgusted at a dinner party with friends: 'Our farts were so smelly we were about to choke. Something had to be done. "Rather than feel sorry for himself, the proactive inventor developed a pill that makes human flatulence as sweet as roses or as seductive as chocolate. And now he sells them online!

16. All right, if you don't want to eat the flatulence

snack, wear the anti-fart underwear and take the scented fart pills, how about natural herbal remedies?

If you prefer to go all "hippie" to deal with your gas problem, natural, earthy substances that decrease the strength of flatulence include peppermint, ginger, yogurt, pumpkin, cardamom and fennel. (source)

17. It is awkwardly easy to fart on aeroplanes.

Due to cabin pressure, more intestinal gas accumulates on an aeroplane than when your feet are firmly planted on solid ground. What's worse, the fact that 50% of the air in the cabin is recirculated means that those stinkers will stay longer than normal.

18. On the other hand, it is impossible to fart in the deep blue sea.

At a depth of 20 or more below sea level the digestive gas stops forming bubbles and instead ignites inside the diver's colon. (source)

19. Members of a South American tribe greet each other by farting.

The Yanomami tribe living in the Amazon rainforest traditionally greet each other with a loud and friendly blast of anal gas.

20. Yes, you disgusting idiot, you can set them on fire.

Is there a more annoying breed of "party guy" than the moron who lights his farts on fire? Of course not! Both methane and hydrogen are flammable, in fact so flammable that a shed full of 90 farting cows caught fire in a German dairy in 2014. But setting your farts on fire during a party is so much fun! We know, but try not to set everything else on fire!

21. Fart inhalation can be healthy.

According to researchers at the University of Exeter, sniffing small amounts of hydrogen sulphide, the gas that makes farts smelly, can reverse mitochondrial damage and help prevent strokes, dementia, cancer and heart attacks.

22. The reason your farts don't smell as bad as everyone else's.

It's the same reason you don't realise that your house smells like your own dog or that you can't smell the rotting hamburger meat that's been stuck behind your fridge for two months: because you're used to it. You 'get used' to the smells, odours and aromas that your own body generates and so you are not as immediately bothered as you would be by the stench from others.

23. Farting among the dead.

For up to three hours after dying and before rigor mortis sets in, dead human bodies are known to continue belching and farting.

24. Tighter anus = louder farts.

If you tend to let out loud farts like a Metallica concert, it just means you don't have a wide open, loose anus that would allow you to let them out much more quietly. So go ahead and be embarrassed that you fart so loudly, but also proud that your anus is tight.

25. *"Professional fart sniffer" is a job in China.*

These smart guys earn up to $50,000 a year diagnosing digestive diseases simply by smelling the patient's flatulence.

26. *Dogs love the smell of farts.*

Although you may probably blame man's best friend when you fart in front of your partner, your dog will never blame you for farting, because they love the aroma of flatulence and will even stick their snout up your ass to get a better sniff.

27. *Termites are the biggest fartists on Earth.*

Those nasty little wood-chewing insects are said to be responsible for a whopping 11% of all methane emissions on the planet - more than cows or humans including vegetarians! According to the EPA:

Global methane emissions from termites are estimated at between 2 and 22 Tg per year, making them the second largest natural source of methane emissions. Methane is produced by termites as part of their normal digestive process and the amount generated varies between species.

Termites are also capable of exploding as suicide bombers with a combination of farts and faeces in a process called 'autotysis'. Scientists have even discovered prehistoric fossil termite farts trapped inside amber.

28. Herrings communicate by farting.

The sweet and tasty sea creature known as the humble herring communicates with other herring through the sounds generated by underwater farts.

29. There is a sea creature that farts in its own mouth.

A pity for the poor Crinoid. Its intestinal tract is U-shaped, which means that its flatulence is released right next to its own mouth.

30. How many farts would it take to make an atomic bomb?

Apparently there are people with so much time on their hands that they can sit around estimating this possibility. One estimate is that a person would have to fart non-stop for six years and nine months to generate the energy of an atomic bomb. Or everyone on Earth would have to fart nine times at once to create a hydrogen bomb.

31. Some people have a fetish for farting.

Although most people recoil at the mere mention of the word "fart," there is a small subgroup of humans who are extremely sexually aroused by flatulence. The fetish is called "eproctophilia".

32. The worst fart foods.

Actually, these are the "best" foods if your goal is to fart more: cruciferous vegetables, eggs, red meat, sorbitol-containing foods, fibre-rich foods, dairy products, garlic and yeast-rich foods. Beans are known to produce flatulence, but they don't tend to generate the sulphur smell of farting.

33. Almost half of all women have farted during sex.

According to a study at the University of California San Francisco-East Bay, 43% of women interviewed reported experiencing "flatulence incontinence" in the previous three months, even though it did not prevent them from having sex.

34. The fabulous rubber toy that imitates farting

In one form or another, toys designed to emulate fart sounds have been around since the Roman Empire, but it wasn't until 1920 that the whoopee cushion was invented to generate mirth and laughter among those who always think farts are hysterical rather than repulsive.

35. *The disturbing proliferation of fake fart apps*

As humans continue to revert even as technology advances, there are at least 60 iPhone apps that recreate the sound of human flatulence.

36. *Flatulence as a defense mechanism*

A psychoanalyst published a study in 1996 on a boy who had been abandoned by his parents and learned to "wrap himself in a protective cloud of familiarity" by repelling potential intruders with the smell of his intestinal gas. The researcher referred to this as "defensive flatulence".

37. *Explosions during intestinal surgery*

The (anal?) annals of science include some cases where the accumulation of intestinal gas during surgery actually led to explosions in the operating theatre.

38. There are hundreds of other terms for "farting".

Such euphemisms include "flatus", "stink", "rectal honk" and "phart".

Fart Jokes and Funny stories

Some people believe that laughing at farts is childish, but we completely disagree. That's why we've found the funniest fart jokes, and we're sharing them below for our readers:

ω *The little old lady is wrong*

A little old lady with all grey hair enters a doctor's office walking briskly. Doctor," she says, "I have a problem with intestinal gas. It doesn't bother me much, because the farts I make are silent and completely odourless. But it does bother me a bit: you see, since I came into your office I've released about twenty farts. Of course, you haven't noticed because they're very quiet and don't stink, but that's how they are. The doctor looks at her and replies: "I understand. I am familiar with this kind of problem. We will do two separate treatments. The first treatment is to take these pills for a week without stopping. Then you will come back to me and we will deal with the second part. After a week, the old lady comes back: "Doctor, I don't know what you gave me to take, but now my farts are still silent, but they have an unbearable stench...!". And the doctor, getting up with a smirk, says "Well, granny. Now that your sinusitis has been cured, let's see what we can do about your hearing!'.

ω   *Carletto hadn't thought of that!*

Carletto has a maniacal passion for borlotti beans, he eats them by the tons. For breakfast, lunch and dinner.

Even his snacks are bean-based. Carletto stuffs himself with these legumes, even though he knows they have devastating effects on him: he farts so much that Zeus' thunder sounds like wet firecrackers.

But one day he meets the woman of his life and, in order not to lose her, he decides to stop eating beans.

For almost a year all goes well, but one evening, on his way back from a business trip, Carletto stops at a restaurant where an unmistakable and irresistible aroma is emanating from. He goes in and stuffs himself with bean soup, borlotti bean salad and bean casserole to the point of overfeeding.

When he gets home, he finds his wife all excited:

"Darling, tonight for dinner there's a nice surprise!"

Carletto is blindfolded, taken into the dining room and made to sit at his usual place. His wife advises him not to take off the blindfold under any circumstances. While he is sitting down, the poor man feels something rising in his belly, but he holds it back. Fortunately the phone rings and his wife runs to answer it.

Carletto takes the opportunity to let out the fart of the century: he raises his little leg and lets out an unbelievable thunderclap, followed by a sigh of relief. The stench is terrifying, Carletto reaches for his napkin to move the air a little, but it's not over yet: an even more devastating super fart is coming out.

He hears his wife talking concisely and takes advantage of it again. The result is worse than the first: a roar of the tenth degree on the Mercalli scale and the pestilential smell of a dead rat.

After a while his wife returns, Carletto pretends not to notice and fixes his napkin on his legs, adopting a delighted expression:

"Darling, did you peek out from under the blindfold?"

"No honey, I swear!"

At this point, his wife took off the blindfold and Carletto found himself in front of a surprise: twenty friends and colleagues, invited for dinner, sitting around him, ready to wish him a happy birthday!

ω   *The weight of farts*

Pierino asks his daddy:

ω   Farting Better   Mao Tze Tze

Dad, dad! Do farts weigh anything?"

"No, Pierino. Why do you ask?"

"Then I crapped my pants!"

ω   The boy who runs

Do you know what a child does when he runs and then stops?

Farts.

ω   Deaf people and farts.

You know why farts stink?

So that even the deaf can hear them.

ω   Grandpa at the table

We are in the countryside, a patriarchal family is sitting around a huge table for dinner.

At the head of the table is the 85-year-old grandfather, who is a bit of a wreck. At a certain point, the old man starts leaning dangerously forward. Everyone starts shouting:

"Ocio, el nono el va, el nono el va!". The father straightens him up and everyone starts eating again.

A few minutes go by and the grandfather begins to lean to the right. There is another shout:

"Ocio! El nono el va! El nono el va!". The father straightens him up again, and dinner resumes.

After a while there is the old man again hanging on the left and everyone shouts again:

"Ocio che el nono el va! El nono el va!".

The father comes up to straighten him up again, but the grandfather looks at him pissed off and starts shouting:

"How come you can't even let out a fart in this house?"

Conclusion

Under normal conditions, most of the gases that form a fart come from our mouths. Only 10% of these gases appear in the fermentation of food along our large intestine. The rest is nothing more than air that we accidentally ingest while eating, or even air bubbles present in saliva or carbonated drinks (mostly soda and beer).

These gases travel through the digestive tract until they discover the gases produced by the effect of bacteria on food. Together, these gases reach the rectal ampulla - the last part of the digestive tract which ends in the anus - and remains compressed until a gap opens to let them out and ruin someone else's day.

This happens 12 to 25 times a day, releasing a total of 1 litre to 1.5 litres of gas. And if you think men fart more than women, you are sadly mistaken. Smell and sound don't choose sex either. Smell depends on what you ate and sound is a combination of factors.

That's not all. We also talked about how to fart more, longer and better. To learn how to get rid of gas and avoid a bloated belly, follow our advice and find out which habits will make a difference to your day.

When food takes longer than normal to digest in the digestive tract, the body begins to eliminate gas and the intestines become more relaxed. So, if you feel imprisoned by your farts, what can you do?

Press your abdomen: lie on your back and, with your knees bent across your stomach, press your abdominal area. This will help to eliminate these gases. Massage your belly with specific movements: move your abdomen from top to bottom in circular movements.

Drink lemon balm tea: it has antispasmodic properties and therefore inhibits the occurrence of stomach spasms. Another good option is ginger tea, because it contains essential oils, such as eugenol, which reduces muscle spasms.

In addition, we talked about the best recipes for creating deadly farts and the best ways to hide your farts.

At this point, you're a fart expert, and you're ready to take on the world, good luck!

From the author <u>Mao Tze Tze</u>:
*the " **Things to Do**" Series*

Instagram channel <u>cose   da   fare</u>
(contact us privately to receive our free products
and previews, or write to
granmaestromaotzetze@gmail.com)